The Gleaming Crest

By Brandon Adamson

Artwork: Mark Schoenecker

Briny Books
Phoenix, AZ 85032

©1995, ©1996,

ISBN-13: 978-0-578-43242-7

Reprint Edition: 2018

Notes:

"Cereal Boy" and "Three Year Reunion" originally
appeared in PLAZM Magazine (1996)

"Mindless Priorities" was published in The
San Fernando Poetry Journal (1996)

The poems "Second Last Show," "Careful Boy," and
"The Replacement" appeared in tight Magazine
literary quarterly (1997)

Dedicated to Mark

The Gleaming Crest

The Gleaming Crest

Alone, embarking on a foolish quest
I commence my search
a solitary soul
confounding the doubt of a forgotten rest

In my half-witted dreams there lies a story
a single obsession
seeking the role of a sentient of glory

My failure induces starvation, despair
lost and distraught
refining a shadow, a soul beyond repair

Here I stand at the foot of a gleaming crest
in a crowded land
a stalwart soul
alone, embarking on my foolish quest

Cereal Boy

Hello.
How are you?
Fine thank you.
Bye.
is the conversation
with an old friend
you see walking down the street whose
personality is like a
bowl of "Alpha-Bits" cereal
that no longer contains alphabet
letters. The letters have been replaced
by something that just doesn't
quite taste the same.

Intelligent Rats

They're after me-
my thoughts,
memories.
Fight 'em-
they fight back
like intelligent rats
determined to overcome the ferocious feline.
Kill 'em-
they won't die
It could never be that simple.
flush them out with alcohol
a good temporary solution.
Hell Yeah
pour myself another drink
and smile as sledgehammers
split my head into spare change
leaving me begging for more of it.

The Lonely Beach

Across the sands of the lonely beach
I wander...

Within the shell of my desolate soul
I ponder...

Imprisoned in the realm of endless futility
I lie

Looking upon the restless, infinite sea
I sigh...

Standing along the shores of shattered glass to be
I weep...

Across the sands of the lonely beach
I sleep...

The Refractor

To offer words of gleam
...refracted
to a whisper
by means of a traitor
himself
...from his words distracted.

Computer Animated Glass Sphere

Who is he?
Who is that guy with the
beanie cap on sitting
inside the glass sphere
in the "Aptiva" commercial?
He makes that thirty second spot
all that it is.
Without him, there is no "Aptiva."
In fact, I would go out and purchase
a big, fat computer
just because of the man crouched
in the glass ball
that is visible for about 2.5 seconds.
He looks like the typical New York
graffiti artist or skater,
disguised as a commercial actor.
He's my hero, a representative
of the modern technological world.

Roaming the Lines

A couple of years ago it
was still safe for one to roam
the lines.
The backtracking of them was only a
minor risk.
Lucky for me.
But now...
the fear of all fears for the shy
components of the adolescent male race
worse than any
murder rate,
deforestation,
global warming,
is the fact that
nearly all girls now have
caller I.D.

The Models

An unseen stranger
detached from all that forget
...yet his ideals
emerging from the shade
amongst the models

Mindless Priorities

Dancing upon the floor of
a sullen battlefield...
preying on the innocent,
while those reluctant to comprehend
...mindless
with their priorities
are fearful of those

...content with themselves

Otters in the Sea

Dreaming of otters in the sea
A solo stranger
Wallowing in an illusion of femininity

Contriving an indelicate course
An unshared outlander
Caressing an image of forbidden discourse

Loathing in an intimate display
An off-colored two-some
Whispering of shadows cast astray

Basking in the light of blithering ecstasy
Forgotten strangers
Dreaming of otters in the sea

The Striped "New Deal" Hat

For years it has rested upon my cranium
with pride,
the "New Deal" beanie,
its crimson and navy blue stripes holding my head,
keeping me from going insane.

Three years ago I bought this
hat the day after the first day I
ever went skateboarding at
"the room"
which is located in the
courthouse parking garage
downtown.

And I've been wearing it ever since.
When they lay me in my coffin
I will be sporting my
striped "New Deal" hat.

Fourteen Candles

Let me tell you how
it feels to be seventeen years
old...

So many damn things in my mind
I don't even know.
Someone should have asked me
when I was fourteen
and knew everything.

Blight Colors

Back in 1993
the best year ever for me
techno, raves, big pants, striped-tees
Tim Gavin shirt with the long sleeves

Hangin' at Club Marilyn
things were much better then.

Bright colors that faded
still wishin' that they stayed

Back in 1993
the best year ever for me

Still Remaining

gazing into the shadowy twilight
one couldn't help but ponder
all the years that had passed
wondering...
what would become of those
still remaining...
seeking answers in the fading twilight
there wasn't much time
Darkness would soon be upon him
...and he knew it.

Three Year Reunion

Hi, is Juliet there?
    Yeah, who's this?
Hey, what's goin' on?
    Not much, who is this?
It's Matt!
    Matt who?
Matt from like, a thousand years ago!
    Oh hey, what's up?
Not much... how'd your Xmas go?
    All right...hung out with the family and stuff
Nice...
    Well hey look, Cameron's on the other line so..
    You can call us later if you want.
Yeah sure.

The Uncertain Order

Regrets occupy the crowded restaurant
of my mind after the waiter comes up,
asks me what I want to order, and I
tell him "nothing" when really I
know exactly what I want, but I'm just
afraid I can't handle the chance of him
serving me the wrong thing
which could easily occur
amidst all the chaos.

If I had another chance I would walk her to her
doorstep, and hopefully she'd take my order.
Now I'll probably never know
because the place in her heart is full
with no room left
for a guy like me.

The Gray File Cabinet

Reflecting the unending grayish
steel which surrounds
itself
with patches of silvery white
light are the bluish gray
elements, easily dazed into such mindless
activities by the
wandering mind
itself.

Untitled

I think I went crazy
a few years back

when all my love trains
    went off track.

Second Last Show

Three years ago today
I was sitting
in this same spot-
a brown plaid armchair leftover
from the seventies. That had to
have been the best night of my entire life-
not the sitting in the chair part,
but that night I went to see a band
play for the second last time, and I met
this girl named Colleen who had a headache
to go with her thin brown hair and eyes
to match. She was sitting underneath the bar and
holding a cup of ice to her head, eyes closed.
After her friends left, that's when
I made my move and sat next
to her- asked if she felt okay....
and BANG! We hit it off. I hardly paid
attention to the music the rest of the
night even though I could barely hear what this
girl was saying due to the extreme loudness. When
the show finally ended, and I arrived
home I caught the name of this
Clint Eastwood movie where a guy named
Lightfoot (played by Jeff Bridges) dies inside
the car from loss of blood or something.
The only reason I would possibly remember that is
because of Colleen. Things never worked out for
us because there was a another guy and because
she broke a bed while playing hide and seek at my
house with him or so she claimed. Yet I can't
help but wonder if right now, three years later,
she's sitting in her favorite chair
thinking about me....
in her boyfriend's apartment.

The Replacement

Last night I met this girl
who looked exactly like
another girl I used to be
in love with named Colleen
At first I thought it was
her younger sister or something
(she did have one,) but the last
name turned out to be different.
We were at this night club (The Mad Planet)
with couches spread out all over
the place. She sat there alone on one
of them. Her friends had all left
her to dance. So I gathered up
every bit of courage I could
muster and proceeded toward the
couch quickly but with caution. I
sat on the couch right next to
her and began to talk...
The first couple of minutes were
rough, and I had a difficult time in my attempts
to break through.
It felt like me doing all the work,
asking questions...

But then the weirdest thing occurred. The
conversation started flowing and
continued to for nearly a half hour.
After a while, her friends
had to leave, so I said goodbye
to her but never asked for her phone number.
Why should I have?
I'll never see her again.

Metropolitan

Staring at colorless images
...all day long
dreaming of solitude
for it is all that is known
to someone
understanding what it means
to see his future
...without knowing.

A Fearless Stare

With foolish eyes, I gaze toward
    beauty I'm unable to face with words
From the obscurity of my desk,
I can't help but stare
    Her angelic blue eyes and flaxen hair
    Shadowed by her crimson glare
Though timid, I'm compulsed to observe
    A feminine body, delicate curves
    Concealed by means of calamitous reserve
Furthermore, my eyes vast and long
    Her satin legs she walks upon
    Shielded by her fearless calm
Perhaps one day I'll attain the fortitude
    Steal her heart and escape from solitude
    If not, my soul may perish soon
With somber eyes I will gaze no more
    Beauty I was unwilling to face with words

12 Hours

My ears hurt the other day
from hearing too much loud music
so I said "huh?"
Then today I spent the first of 12
picking up a copy of some of it
a cd
because a girl at a concert told me
I looked like the singer from Bush
but I don't-
except for maybe the eyes-
when I squint.
Maybe it could have just been
a pick up line-if I were lucky-
but I never am.
...So 8 to 8, an awfully long time
for a young man to roam-
but not enough for me.
Next stop,
The Landmark of the hours
I'll likely spend a couple there
Moving on to caffeine and
the Prospects of a mall-
whose pay phone number I know by heart
and that will protect me from
the remaining hours of the days youth.

Careful Boy

I want to go up and talk to that girl
She looks kinda fresh
    No, you can't...
Why not? You know her?
    Yeah. You have to be careful..she's not a girl
    you can just approach and
    be all "ha ha nation known!..."
What's her name?
    Mandy.
Isn't she from 'tosa?
    Yeah.
Now I have to go talk to her.
    Just be careful...she's not a normal
    girl...You don't know her story...
Tell me her story.
    I'll tell you later...Now's your chance,
    she's all alone.
All right. I've got a line.

    You want to sell that sweatshirt?
    I'll give you 20 bucks for it right now.
I can't. It isn't mine.
    Whose is it?
My boyfriend's!
    Who's he?
Jason (last name something hard to pronounce.)
    Does he go to East?
He's twenty one.
    Oh...do you know blah blah blah?
Yeah I know her. Do you know blah blah blah?
    Of course.
It's my birthday tomorrow.
    What do you want for your birthday?
Nothing. I got a car.

    Mandy, we're ready to leave this place,
    you coming?
I'll meet you guys there.

Anyways...
  Yeah, anyways.
I guess I have to go.
  Yeah. What did you say your name was again?
  Matt.
Matt who?
  Nation known Matt.
Oh, okay.
  See you around.

I can't believe you actually did it!
You just went up and talked to her.
You get mad props for that.

So tell me her story. Now I have to hear it.
I'll tell you in the car. Let's go.
Yeah, nothing left for me in here.

Diamond Poems

food
yummy good
eating chewing chomping
bananas eggs steak chicken
cold wet
water

car
fast loud
riding driving racing
stereo wheels seats stick
fast big
plane

toilet
dirty filthy
flushing overflowing cleaning
excretion cleaner bacteria water
sturdy easy
sink

Shuttle Run

Hangin' with 10 inch at shuttle
Finding some new kind of trouble
Gay guy refills the Diet Coke
A sketch feeling fills my throat

Went searching for love at Mayfair
Found some girls that didn't play fair
Had to watch where I could walk
Trying to prove I'm not 10 stalks

Trouble started at the food court
Didn't care what I was in for
When Beater met Lois Lane
I couldn't let it end that day

The one I liked the most was Mandy
The one that can't remember me
Finest girl in the 'tosa crew
She'll love me before I'm through

Life as a Beater is a hard one
All the mean girls make things fun

The Land of the Sullen

The valley in the sun
Awaiting...
Sweltering in a mindless blight
self-loathing...
Pondering a shady retreat

From the land of the sullen...
        to the valley in the sun.

About the Author

Brandon Adamson is a poet and nation known rockstar who resides in Phoenix, Arizona.